GRADE

8

The 2005 & 2006 Syllabus shoul[
requirements, especially those fo[
sight-reading. Attention should [
Notices on the inside front cover, v[
any changes.

The syllabus is obtainable from music retailers or from the Services Department, The Associated Board of the Royal Schools of Music, 24 Portland Place, London W1B 1LU, United Kingdom (please send a stamped addressed C5 (162mm x 229mm) envelope).

In exam centres outside the UK, information and syllabuses may be obtained from the Local Representative.

GW00363598

CONTENTS
page

Where appropriate, pieces in this volume have been checked with original source material and edited as necessary for instructional purposes. Any editorial additions to the texts are given in small print, within square brackets, or – in the case of slurs and ties – in the form ⌢. Fingering, phrasing, pedalling, metronome marks and the editorial realization of ornaments (where given) are for guidance only; they are not comprehensive or obligatory.

Editor for the Associated Board: **Richard Jones**

DO NOT
PHOTOCOPY
© MUSIC

Alternative pieces for this grade

Music origination by Barnes Music Engraving Ltd.
Cover by Økvik Design.
Printed in England by Headley Brothers Ltd,
The Invicta Press, Ashford, Kent.

Allemande

Second movement from Partita No. 4 in D, BWV 828

Edited by
Walter Emery

J. S. BACH

Partita No. 4 in D, BWV 828, was first published in 1728 and then reappeared within a collected edition of six partitas, or suites, in 1731. According to the original title-page, the partitas were 'composed for music-lovers, to delight their spirits'. The traditional dance types are very freely handled, and here the allemande is no longer recognizably a dance but rather the vehicle for a sustained, florid, lyrical right-hand 'solo', supported by twinned left-hand parts. Dynamics are left to the player's discretion. The chords in bb. 1, 25 and 26 might be spread, as they would be in a harpsichord performance. Walter Emery suggests that the tied right-hand note in the middle of b. 14 (and in the parallel bb. 15, 33 and 34) might be ornamented as follows:

Source: *Clavier Übung*, Op. 1 (Leipzig, 1731)

4

Prelude and Fugue in E flat

No. 19 from *24 Preludes and Fugues*, Op. 87

A:2

SHOSTAKOVICH

Dmitry Shostakovich (1906–75) wrote his *24 Preludes and Fugues*, Op. 87, as a tribute to J. S. Bach. They were composed in 1950–51 after a visit to Leipzig occasioned by the bicentenary of Bach's death. Like *The Well-Tempered Clavier*, Shostakovich's collection includes a prelude and fugue in every key, but whereas Bach's key order is chromatic, Shostakovich's is cyclical, ascending through the entire circle of fifths.

Fugue a 3

Moderato con moto ($\bullet$ = 144)

A:3

Sonata in D

Kp. 535

D. SCARLATTI

Domenico Scarlatti (1685–1757), Neapolitan by birth, emigrated to Spain in 1728 and spent the rest of his life at the Spanish court. The vast majority of his nearly 600 solo keyboard sonatas – mostly single-movement binary pieces – belong to these years. Scarlatti's own description of his music in the preface to the *Essercizi* (30 sonatas) of 1738 is no less apt for the late sonatas such as Kp. 535: 'In these compositions, do not expect any profound learning, but rather an ingenious jesting with art.' Dynamics are left to the player's discretion.
Source: Parma XV (1757) 22

Allegro assai

First movement from Sonata in F minor, H. 173, Wq. 57/6

Edited by
Howard Ferguson

C. P. E. BACH

Taught by his father, Bach's second son Carl Philipp Emanuel (1714–88) became a professional keyboard player, serving for many years as harpsichordist to Frederick the Great in Berlin. He composed over 350 works for solo keyboard and wrote one of the most influential treatises of the 18th century, the *Versuch über die wahre Art das Clavier zu spielen* (Essay on the True Art of Playing Keyboard Instruments, Berlin, 1753–62). In this fast movement the fingering is mostly the composer's. Howard Ferguson suggests that the dotted rhythms might be articulated as follows throughout: etc. The tricky ornaments in bb. 2, 12, 36 and 66 might be abbreviated to

Source: *Clavier-Sonaten nebst einigen Rondos fürs Forte-piano für Kenner und Liebhaber… dritte Sammlung* (Leipzig, 1781)

Reproduced from C. P. E. Bach: *Selected Keyboard Works*, Book III, edited by Howard Ferguson (Associated Board)

Allegro moderato

First movement from Sonata in C, K. 330/300h

MOZART

The Sonata in C, K. 330, 'one of the most lovable works Mozart ever wrote', according to Alfred Einstein, is the first of a group of three (K. 330–32) composed around 1781–3 in Munich or Vienna and published as a set in 1784. Of the first movement Denis Matthews has written: 'The added word "moderato" should be a safeguard against playing [it] too fast…the tempo in fact hovers on the border between two and four-in-a-bar.' He adds that pedalling should be used sparingly. As an alternative ornament realization in b. 2, the closing notes (*d" e"*) might be taken into the trill.
Sources: autograph MS, formerly in the Berlin Staatsbibliothek; original edition, *Trois sonates pour le clavecin ou pianoforte* (Vienna: Artaria, 1784)

Adapted from Mozart: *Sonatas for Pianoforte*, Vol. II, edited by Stanley Sadie and Denis Matthews (Associated Board)

24

27

AB 2984

B:3

Sonata in E minor, Op. 90

First movement

BEETHOVEN

Mit Lebhaftigkeit und durchaus mit Empfindung und Ausdruck [♩. = c.48]
[With animation, and always with feeling and expression]

The Sonata in E minor, Op. 90, was written in the summer of 1814 and already foreshadows the greater density and concentration of Beethoven's late style. The composer decisively turns his back on convention in adopting German tempo marks exclusively for the first time, in avoiding an exposition repeat, and in blurring the divisions between exposition and development (bb. 79–85) and between development and recapitulation

(bb. 130–44). Beethoven described the first movement as 'a contest between head and heart'. Tovey characterized it as 'a movement full of passionate and lonely energy' and warned that the tempo must be kept uniform (*Sonatas for Pianoforte*, Vol. III, Associated Board). Of the left-hand chords in bb. 17 and 21 he wrote: 'If you cannot stretch the 10th, be careful to put its bass-note on the beat (and within the pedal) regardless of the delay to the rest of the chord'; and of b. 138: 'Put the RH on the edge of the keys and keep it there below the LH.'

In some editions the passages at bb. 18–19, 161–2 and 239–40 have the same crescendo and diminuendo markings each time; on the third beat of b. 119 the LH *G♯* is tied to the *G♯* at the beginning of b. 120; and at b. 143 the third beat is a chord, as at the start.

Source: *Sonate für das Piano-forte*, Op. 90 (Vienna: S. A. Steiner, 1815)

C:1

Impromptu

No. 1 from *Quatre morceaux pour piano*, Op. 25

ARENSKY

The Russian composer, conductor and pianist Anton Stepanovich Arensky (1861–1906) studied composition with Rimsky-Korsakov at the St Petersburg Conservatory from 1879 to 1882. He was then appointed professor of harmony and counterpoint at the Moscow Conservatory, numbering among his pupils Rachmaninoff, Skryabin and Glière. In the Impromptu many left-hand chords involving intervals of a 10th or more from b. 3 onwards will need to be spread. In the middle section, between b. 26 and b. 41, the dynamics will have to be supplemented by the player.

Source: *Impromptu*, Op. 25 No. 1 (London: Augener, 1913)

Autumn Crocus

C:2

MAYERL

Billy Joseph Mayerl (1902–59) was an English pianist and composer who built a career in music hall and music theatre and became an acknowledged master of light music. He wrote some 300 short piano pieces, often named after flowers.

AB 2984

Moderato grazioso

C:3

Intermezzo

No. 4 from *Faschingsschwank aus Wien*, Op. 26

SCHUMANN

The first four movements of *Faschingsschwank aus Wien* were composed in March 1839 in Vienna, where Schumann then intended to settle with Clara Wieck, whom he married the following year. The fifth and last movement followed a few months later, after his return to Leipzig. Schumann himself described the work as 'a great romantic sonata'. The title may be translated as 'Carnival Jest from Vienna' – the jest is the reference in the opening movement to the *Marseillaise*, which was then banned in Vienna for political reasons.

Since Schumann's metronome marks are notoriously unreliable, and that for the Intermezzo (♩ = 116) seems impossibly fast, an editorial metronome mark has been given here instead. In the absence of an initial dynamic mark, *f* (or at least *mf*) may be assumed. Howard Ferguson points out that the two-bar stretches of unchanged pedal at bb. 14–15 and 29–30 require half-pedalling if the low bass octave is to be sustained without confusing the changing harmonies of the upper parts. The LH semiquaver at the end of bb. 14 and 29 coincides in the source with the last RH triplet-semiquaver, which is presumably how it should be played. The LH crotchet rests are quaver rests in the source.

Source: *Faschingsschwank aus Wien: Fantasiebilder für das Piano-Forte* (Vienna: Mechetti, 1841)

Adapted from Schumann: *Faschingsschwank aus Wien*, Op. 26, edited by Howard Ferguson (Associated Board)

48

50

AB 2984

Dem Andenken Petöfis

LISZT

Dem Andenken Petöfis (In Memory of Petöfi) is a late work, written in 1877, not long after Liszt had been appointed the first president of the newly formed National Hungarian Royal Academy of Music. The piece is an elegy – of which there are many among Liszt's piano works – written in memory of the Hungarian poet Sándor Petöfi, whose poems Liszt occasionally set to music.
Source: *Dem Andenken Petöfi's: Melodie… für Pianoforte* (Budapest, 1877)

© 2004 by The Associated Board of the Royal Schools of Music

Bagatelle No. 3

C:5

RAWSTHORNE

The English composer Alan Rawsthorne (1905–71) entered the Royal Manchester College of Music in 1925, studying piano and cello. From 1932 he taught at Dartington Hall School, but after the Second World War devoted himself almost entirely to composition. His chief solo piano works are the four Bagatelles (1938), the Sonatina (1949), the *Four Romantic Pieces* (1953) and the Ballade (1967).

56

Romance

C:6

TAKEMITSU

The Japanese composer Tōru Takemitsu (1930–96) was largely self-taught, numbering Debussy and Messiaen among his chief influences. The *Romance* is his earliest published piano piece, dating from 1949.

(espress. cantando)

60

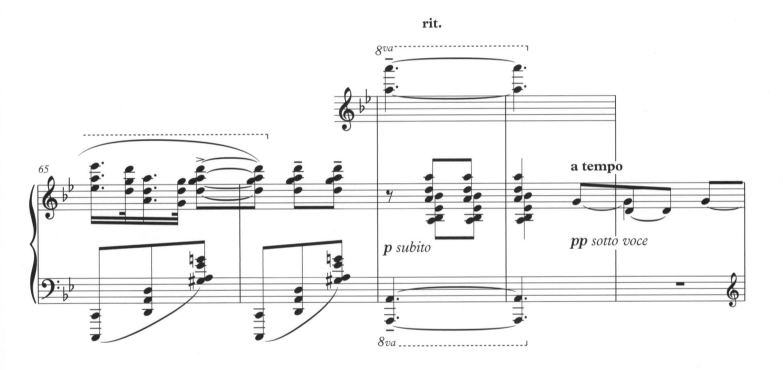